SOCIAL STUDIES MATTERS!

WHAT IS CIVICS?

PETER FINN

PowerKiDS press

Published in 2024 by The Rosen Publishing Group, Inc.
2544 Clinton Street, Buffalo, NY 14224

Copyright © 2024 by The Rosen Publishing Group, Inc.

All rights reserved. No part of this book may be reproduced in any form without permission in writing from the publisher, except by a reviewer.

Editor: Therese Shea
Book Design: Michael Flynn

Photo Credits: Cover, p. 1 Joaquin Corbalan P/Shutterstock.com; (series background) Eky Studio/Shutterstock.com; p. 5 glenda/Shutterstock.com; p. 7 Aaron of L.A. Photography/Shutterstock.com; p. 9 Ground Picture/Shutterstock.com; p. 11 Andrey_Popov/Shutterstock.com; p. 13 LightField Studios/Shutterstock.com; p. 15 Joseph Sohm/Shutterstock.com; p. 17 Jeff McCollough/Shutterstock.com; p. 19 Jacob Lund/Shutterstock.com; p. 21 PeopleImages.com - Yuri A/Shutterstock.com.

Library of Congress Cataloging-in-Publication Data

Names: Finn, Peter, 1978- author.
Title: What is civics? / Peter Finn.
Description: Buffalo, New York : PowerKids Press, [2024] | Series: Social studies matters! | Includes bibliographical references and index.
Identifiers: LCCN 2023026556 (print) | LCCN 2023026557 (ebook) | ISBN 9781499443837 (library binding) | ISBN 9781499443820 (paperback) | ISBN 9781499443844 (ebook)
Subjects: LCSH: Civics–Juvenile literature. | Citizenship–United States–Juvenile literature.
Classification: LCC JK1759 .F46 2024 (print) | LCC JK1759 (ebook) | DDC 320.473–dc23/eng/20230622
LC record available at https://lccn.loc.gov/2023026556
LC ebook record available at https://lccn.loc.gov/2023026557

Manufactured in the United States of America

Some of the images in this book illustrate individuals who are models. The depictions do not imply actual situations or events.

CPSIA Compliance Information: Batch #CWPK24. For Further Information contact Rosen Publishing at 1-800-237-9932

CONTENTS

Pledging Allegiance. 4
What Is Civics? 6
Rights. 8
Responsibilities 10
Who Is a Citizen? 12
Naturalization 14
Losing Citizenship. 16
Civics Is Important!. 18
Young Citizens 20
Glossary 22
For More Information 23
Index 24

Pledging Allegiance

"I pledge **allegiance** to the flag of the United States of America." Do you say this pledge, or promise, at school? If you do, you're promising to be **loyal** to the flag and to the United States. Loyalty is a duty of U.S. citizens.

What Is Civics?

Citizens are full members of a country. They have certain rights. They are fully **protected** by their country's laws. Citizens also have duties to their country. The study of the rights and duties of citizens is called civics.

Rights

The rights and **responsibilities** of citizens are different in each country. In many countries, citizens have the right to vote. They may have the right to speak freely and without fear of **punishment**. Not all countries give these rights to citizens, though.

Responsibilities

Citizens have responsibilities too. In the United States and Canada, paying taxes is a duty. So is serving on a **jury** when needed. In some countries, citizens must serve in the military for a time. Many think voting is both a right and a duty.

Who Is a Citizen?

In many countries, anyone born in that country receives citizenship. Having a mother or father who is a citizen often means their child is a citizen of that same country. People sometimes become citizens of a country by marrying a citizen.

Naturalization

People can go through a **process** called naturalization to become citizens too. This process is different in each country. People often have to live in their new country for a time. They may need to pass a test about the country's laws and history too.

Losing Citizenship

Sometimes, people must give up citizenship in one country to become citizens of another. But sometimes they can be citizens of two countries at once. People can also have citizenship taken away. That might happen if they vote in another country's elections.

17

Civics Is Important!

Citizens should know their rights and their duties. They can decide if they want changes in their country. They can ask for those changes. They can run for office too. That means trying to get **elected** to a government job.

Young Citizens

Some citizens aren't old enough to vote or run for office. They can still practice good citizenship. They can follow the laws. They can help others in their community. They can learn about their country in school. A good country is full of good citizens!

GLOSSARY

allegiance: Loyalty to a person, group, or cause.

elect: To choose for a position in a government.

jury: A group of people who are chosen to make a decision in a case in a court of law.

loyal: Faithful.

process: A series of steps or actions taken to complete something.

protect: To keep safe.

punishment: The penalty for a fault or crime.

responsibility: A duty or task that someone is required or expected to do.

FOR MORE INFORMATION

BOOKS
Brown, Liz. *Civics*. New York, NY: AV² by Weigl, 2020.

Lawton, Cassie M. *Rights and Responsibilities.* New York, NY: Cavendish Square Publishing, 2021.

Price-Wright, Heather. *Talking About Civics.* Huntington Beach, CA: Teacher Created Materials, 2022.

WEBSITES

Becoming a U.S. Citizen
www.ducksters.com/history/us_government/becoming_a_us_citizen.php
Discover what the U.S. naturalization process is like. See if you can answer some of the questions that people are asked.

Citizenship
kids.britannica.com/kids/article/citizenship/399912#
Read more about the duties and rights of citizens of different countries.

Publisher's note to educators and parents: Our editors have carefully reviewed these websites to ensure that they are suitable for students. Many websites change frequently, however, and we cannot guarantee that a site's future contents will continue to meet our high standards of quality and educational value. Be advised that students should be closely supervised whenever they access the internet.

INDEX

C
Canada, 10
citizenship, 12, 16, 20
civics, 6
community, 20

D
duties, 4, 6, 10, 18

G
government, 18

J
jury, 10

L
laws, 6, 14, 20
loyalty, 4

M
military, 10

N
naturalization, 14

R
responsibilities, 8, 10

T
taxes, 10

U
United States, 4, 10

V
voting, 8, 10, 16, 20